Letter Composed During a Lull in the Fighting

ALSO BY KEVIN POWERS
The Yellow Birds

Letter Composed During a Lull in the Fighting

Poems

KEVIN POWERS

Little, Brown and Company

New York   Boston   London

Little, Brown and Company
Hachette Book Group
237 Park Avenue, New York, NY 10017
littlebrown.com

First Edition: April 2014

Little, Brown and Company is a division of Hachette Book Group, Inc. The Little, Brown name and logo are trademarks of Hachette Book Group, Inc.

The publisher is not responsible for websites (or their content) that are not owned by the publisher.

The Hachette Speakers Bureau provides a wide range of authors for speaking events. To find out more, go to hachettespeakersbureau.com or call (866) 376-6591.

The following poems were originally published (some in slightly differently form) in the following publications:

"Letter Composed During a Lull in the Fighting" in *Poetry Magazine*, 2009
"While Trying to Make an Arrowhead in the Fashion of the Mattaponi
    Indians" in *Cream City Review*, 2009
"Separation" in *The New York Quarterly*, Issue 66, 2010
"Great Plain" and "Field Manual" in *The Sun*, 2010
"Cumberland Gap," "Songs in Planck Time," "The Torch and Pitchfork
    Blues," and "The Abhorrence of Coincidence" in *diode*, 2011
"Death, Mother and Child" and "After Leaving McGuire Veterans' Hospital
    for the Last Time" in *Hayden's Ferry Review*, 2012
"The Locks of the James" in *Huck*, 2013

ISBN 978-0-316-40108-1
LCCN 2014931143

10 9 8 7 6 5 4 3 2 1

RRD-C

Book design by Marie Mundaca

Printed in the United States of America

For my friends from the Boulevard

CONTENTS

ONE

Customs

Amen may have meant "to begin"
back then. So be it, the desert, I imagine,
said. So be it, as the car I'm traveling in
turns right on state highway 71,
due west into the vast unending waste
of Texas.

Now it only lets us know that things are at an end,
among them is the sun hung out
to dry any echo of my voice that would survive
the turbines' spinning blades
as we drift through the windmill field
and on into Old Mexico.

We passed the welcome sign
five miles ago. Another crossing
missed. On some naked mountainside
a small signal fire is lit. I can tell you exactly

what I mean. It is night again and endless
are the stars. I can tell you exactly
what I mean. The world has been replaced
by our ideas about the world.

Letter Composed During a Lull in the Fighting

I tell her I love her like not killing
or ten minutes of sleep
beneath the low rooftop wall
on which my rifle rests.

I tell her in a letter that will stink,
when she opens it,
of bolt oil and burned powder
and the things it says.

I tell her how Private Bartle says, offhand,
that war is just us
making little pieces of metal
pass through each other.

Great Plain

Here is where appreciation starts, the boy
in a dusty velour tracksuit almost getting shot.
When I say boy, I mean it. When I say almost
getting shot, I mean exactly that. For bringing
unexploded mortars right up to us
takes a special kind of courage I don't have.
A dollar for each one, I'm told,
on orders from brigade HQ
to let the children do the dirty work.

When I say, I'd say fuck that, let the bastards find them
with the heels of boots and who cares if I mean us
as bastards and who cares if heels of boots mean things
that once were, the way grass once was a green thing
and now is not, the way the muezzin call once was
five times today and now is not

and when I say heel of boot I hope you'll appreciate
that I really mean the gone foot, any one of us

timbered and inert and when I say green
I mean like fucking Nebraska, wagon wheels on the prairie
and other things that can't be appreciated
until you're really far away and they come up
as points of reference.

I don't know what Nebraska looks like.
I've never been. When I say Nebraska
I mean the idea of, the way an ex-girlfriend of mine
once talked about the idea of a gun. But guns are not ideas.
They are not things to which comparisons are made. They
    are

one weight in my hand when the little boy crests the green
    hill
and the possibilities of shooting him or not extend out
    from me
like the spokes of a wheel. The hills are not green anymore
and in my mind they never were, though when I say they
    were
I mean I'm talking about reality. I appreciate that too,

knowing
the hills were green,
knowing
someone else has paid him
for his scavenging, one less

exploding thing beneath our feet.
I appreciate the fact
that for at least one day I don't have to decide
between dying and shooting a little boy.

Inheritance

It is useful to be in love
with useless things.
The old pear cactuses that withered
in our yard when we were young,
I loved. Among other things, I loved
the clear glass bottle of
Old Milwaukee that you threw
from the window of your car
into the garbage can
when you came home,
loved the way it broke
into a dozen broken pieces
and the way a dozen more
surrounded them
like constellations, loved
what dignity there seemed to be
in the way that any single thing that orbits
gives up on being more
than needed for a while.
Once I loved an old man, too,

who had no use for useless things,
like this poem, which might
be out there spinning
with him anyway.

Blue Star Mother

Compare my sins to this, for instance,
my mother refusing to have her picture taken,
always raising up her hands the moment that
the shutter clicks, so that looking back
on the photographic
evidence of my life
one could be easily convinced
I was raised by a woman
whose face was the palm of a hand.

This is not the case. I know that
in the seventies she wore
large glasses, apparently sat often enough
on cheap imitation teak couches
to be photographed on them more than once, sometimes
had her hair done up
in whatever fashion
wives of factory workers

wore in Richmond
and was beautiful.

But after hanging her blue star up she covered it
with curtains. She stopped
going to the hairdresser
and took up gardening instead.
Which is to say that when she woke up
in the middle of the night
she'd stand in the yard in her nightgown
staring at a clump of dead azaleas
running down beside the house.
Later, she stopped sleeping.
Later still, her hair went grey.

I had a picture of her
in my helmet, shuffled in
with other pictures.
I think it was in between
some cutouts from
a *Maxim* magazine and
a Polaroid of my girlfriend's tits
with a note on it that said,
Sorry, last one, be safe, XOXO.

My mother told me
about a dream she had

before the sleeping stopped. I died
and woke her at her bedside
to tell her I was dead,
though I would not have
had to tell her because
I'd already bled on her favorite floral rug
and half my jaw was missing.
I don't know what to make of that.

I like to think she caught
some other mother's dream,
because she could take
how hard the waiting was,
and had all that practice
getting up her hands.

Independence Day

Sunset: the shadow of the carillon
had done its covering of us.
The girl with red hair finally turned toward me
and the blanket and the grass and the white oaks
smelled like the furthest thing from memory I
could have asked for.

And the ringing I
did not hear next did not come from the building's bells,
but from the sound
of each ignited shell
that boxed my ears with its beginning. I
began to shake and I
saw the girl with red hair's eyes
and that she saw me
shake and the mouths of whole families
gone wide and rounded in amazement.

I do not believe in silence.
There is no such thing.

But I
believed the woman in Ward C of McGuire veterans'
   hospital
who told me to dig
my feet into the ground as hard as I
could if I
ever doubted
the firmness of reality.

And I
had practiced digging down
and down into the earth
with my hands
with my elbows
with my body
with my eyes
gone wide, in fact I
have tried to become earth
many times, to be lower than earth, and I
have known many boys
who practiced it so much
that they stayed below the surface.

So I dig my heels into the green grass, wearing out
the blanket and the carillon's lawn and
I shake, turning

to the girl with red hair,
grasping her waist,
until lastly
we reach resonance.

Valentine with Flat Affect

Everybody knows
the number of things to be in love with
is reducing
at a rate more or less equal to
the expansion of the universe.

This is called entropy, I think.
Some things are, however, left:
you, in that gingham dress,
for one, for which
I will not apologize
to anyone for loving.

Other aspects of a life become prioritized
by chance, and our mistake
is that we guess that every ground must break
along the fault
that it is given.

So no, I don't care as much
about the fish I pulled
out of the river in a net as I do
you. Most
of what I catch slips back
between

the empty spaces in the old net
anyway. It's hard enough to find
my footing, let alone
decide what to call remarkable,
and not just because I am fed
and clothed and not unreasonably
happy.

Elegy for Urgency

Sometimes, when the wind blows so certainly
you feel that it is spring, regardless of the season,
there is no cause to comment on it. It goes,
and if it passes over a child
in a carriage at the end of the sidewalk,
you would be forgiven for not noticing
the one moment in your life
you were allowed to see the holy.

But you have noticed nothing in a long time,
holy or otherwise, so it is not remarkable
that you spent the rest of the day listening blankly
as your friends and loved ones chattered on,
unable even to speak,
the whole time dizzying further, only aware
of the futility of trying to fix yourself in the world
with words you cannot remember.

The names of the trees are trees
and birds are those singing things

carrying their music off to a place
to which you've lost the way.
If your hands were not clasped together
you could spread out your palms
and hope that some song might fall
down into them. You've tried.
If only you could recall the name,
which you are sure is resting
right there on the tip of your tongue
with the rest of your life.

Meditation on a Main Supply Route

I recall Route Tampa going on
in a straight line all the way
out of the war.
A hundred MSRs
with names once so unpronounceable
they are now called Chevy and Toyota;
their attendant smells
and voices arrive
in such disparate places
as Danville, Virginia;
Monterey, California;
Steubenville, Ohio;
Weslaco, Texas;
Fayettevilles
of both North Carolina
and of Arkansas;
the Bronx, New York,
where Curtis Jefferson's
cauterized face still burns
as he wraps his lips

around a straw to drink his juice
and his muscles wither and he wishes
he had died instead of living
houseboundbedboundmindboundbodybound
like a child, watching
as his mother watched
the roads, pitted and seeded,
arrive as one road in front of his house,
get out of a black sedan
with GOVERNMENT USE license plates
and become two men
walking up the front steps
of the converted brownstone,
where they wait. And the roads
reach out to Steven Abernathy
in the factory where he works,
after, on C shift, forever, and Steven
saying to the old intractable drunks he works with
that all pain is phantom and that's all
as he cleats the red knuckle of his leg
into the stirrup above the plastic rest of it,
before they take him to the VFW post
for a PBR on them at least twice a week,
now almost daily for a month,
arriving in the glare of six a.m. light
off the quarter panels of their rusted trucks.
Sometimes by noon the old men say Vietnam

and he says, I lost my leg
on the goddamn MSR and old Earl Yates says,
Naw, they took it, the fuckers.

I am home and whole, so to speak.
The streetlights are in place along the avenue
just as I remembered
and just as I remember
there is tar slick on the poles
because it has rained. It doesn't matter.
I know these roads will work
their way to me. They may arrive
right here, at this small circle of light
folding in on itself where brick
and broken sidewalk meet.
So, I must be prepared. But I can't remember
how to be alive. It has begun
to rain so hard I fear I'll drown.
I guess we ought to
take these pennies off our eyes,
strike into them new likenesses;
toss them with new wishes
into whatever water can be found.

TWO

Improvised Explosive Device

The blast from an improvised explosive device moves at 13,000 mph, gets as hot as 7,000 degrees and creates 400 tons of pressure per square inch. "No one survives that. We're trying to save the kids at 25 meters and beyond."

—Ronald Glasser in the *Army Times*

If this poem had wires
coming out of it,
you would not read it.
If the words in this poem were made
of metal, if you could see
the mechanics of their curvature,
you would hope
they would stay covered
by whatever paper rested
in the trash pile they were hidden in.
But words or wires would lead you still
to fields of grass between white buildings.

If this poem were made of metal and you read it, if you did
decide to read or hear the words, you would see wires
where there were none,
you would pick up the slack of words, you would reel
them in, pull
loose lines
until you stood in that dry field,
where you'd sweat. You would wonder how you looked
from rooftop level, if you had been targeted.
If these words were buried beneath debris, you would
ask specific questions, like, am I in a field of words?
What will happen if they are unearthed?
Is the entire goddamn country full of them?
Prefer that they be words, not wires, not made of metal,
which is almost always trouble. If these words should lead you
to the rough center of a field,
you'll stand half-blind
from the bright light off white buildings,
still holding the slack line in your hand,
wondering if you have been chosen.
You'll realize that you both have been and not,
and that an accident is as much of a choice
as saying, "I am going to read this poem."

If this poem had wires coming out of it,
you would call the words devices,

if you found them threatening in any way,
for ease of communication
and because you would marvel
at this new, broad category.
This is another way of saying
we'd rely on jargon to understand each other,
like calling a year a tour,
even though there are never any women
in bustled dresses carrying umbrellas
to protect complexions. In moments
you might think these words were grand,
in an odd way, never imagining you would
find a need to come back to them,
or that you'd find days
that you were desperate
for the potential of metal,
wires, and hidden things.

And if this poem was somehow traveling
with you
in the turret of a Humvee,
you would not see the words
buried at the edges of the road.
You would not see the wires. You would not
see the metal. You would not see the danger
in the architecture
of a highway overpass.

If this poem has left you deaf,
if the words in it are smoking,
if parts of it have passed through your body
or the bodies of those you love, this will go a long way
toward explaining why you will, in later years,
prefer to sleep on couches. If these words have caused
casualties, then this poem will understand
that, oftentimes, to be in bed
is to be one too many layers
away from wakefulness.

If this poem was made of words
the sergeant said — after, like, don't
worry boys, it's war, it happens —
as the cab filled up with opaque smoke
and laughter, then it would be natural
for you to think of rote — *rauta*,
the old Norse called it, the old
drumbeat of break of wave
on shore — as an analogue
for the silence that has filled your ears
again
and particles of light
funneled through the holes
made by metal meeting metal
meeting muscle meeting bone.

You would not see. You would not hear. You would not
be blamed for losing focus for a second: this poem
does not come with an instruction manual. These words
do not tell you how to handle them.
You would not be blamed
for what they'd do if they were metal,
or for after taking aim at a man holding a telephone in his
    hand
in an alley. You would not be blamed for thinking
words could have commanded it.

If this poem had fragments
of metal coming out of it, if these words were your best
    friend's legs,
dangling, you might not care or even wonder whether
or not it was only the man's mother on the other end
of the telephone line. For one thing, it would be
exonerating. Secondly, emasculating (in the metaphorical
sense of male powerlessness, notwithstanding the
    likelihood
that the mess the metal made of your friend's legs and
    trousers
has left more than that detached). If this poem had wires
    for words,
you would want someone to pay.

If this poem had wires coming out of it,
you wouldn't read it.
If these words were made of metal
they could kill us all. But these
are only words. Go on,
they are safe to fold and put into your pocket.
Even better, they are safe
to be forgotten.

Self-Portrait in Sidewalk Chalk

Once, when seeing
my shadow on the ground
I tried to outline it
in chalk. It kept moving
as I knelt, and as the sun
moved itself from horizon
to horizon, the chalk
was changed.

It ranged from arm
to curve of elbow,
from my altered
organs to the shadow
that a church bell cast
beneath the movement
of the sun.

It finally fell
and evening came
and dark spread

into the wide world.
My shadow disappeared,
disloyal, and the chalk
showed only myself
strapped monstrously
into a chair.

A History of Yards

My mother, in the porch light, sets out
two tea services in the tilted dirt
of her yard, gently rests the porcelain cups
and saucers in two places near level, seems
not to be watching the bloom of azaleas
first submission to air, but is and has been.

I am far from her. Not hearing the mortars
descending and knowing no way of explaining
what it means to be mortared, I lie
in a courtyard eight thousand miles distant
and remember she's watching as she has been
each morning since I promised not to die.

I open my body. She shakes out the heat
of the kettle, watches steam rise; ascending, diffusing —
she cannot tell and would not if she could, and remains
in the soil in the four a.m. air beneath six rows
of dogwoods and watches two blooms in one moment:

mine, in the dust. She is driving her body
beneath the soil of her garden
as far as she can, not knowing I never
took cover; ears already ringing
yet somehow still hearing her voice
that I held as a child saying *never be afraid*

to love everything. She, beneath
the porch light, watches
my body open,
the daylight becoming equal to it.

Death, Mother and Child

Mosul, Iraq, 2004

Kollwitz was right. Death is an etching.
I remember the white Opel being
pulled through the traffic circle on the back of a wrecker,
the woman in the driver's seat
so brutalized by bullets it was hard to tell her sex.
Her left arm waved unceremoniously
in the stifling heat and I retched,
the hand seemingly saying, *I will see
you there.* We heard a rumor that a child
was riding in the car with her, had slipped
to the floorboard, but had been killed as well.
The truth has no spare mercy, see. It is this chisel
in the woodblock. It is this black wisp
above the music of a twice-rung bell.

Field Manual

Think not of battles, but rather after,
when the tremor in your right leg
becomes a shake you cannot stop, when the burned man's
tendoned cheeks are locked into a scream that,
before you sank the bullet in his brain to end it,
had been quite loud. Think of how he still seems to scream.
Think of not caring. Call this "relief."

Think heat waves rising from the dust.
Think days of rest, how the sergeant lays
the .22 into your palm and says the dogs
outside the wire have become a threat
to good order and to discipline:
some boys have taken them as pets, they spread
disease, they bit a colonel preening for a TV crew.

Think of afternoons in T-shirt and shorts,
the unending sun, the bite of sweat in eyes.

Think of missing so often it becomes absurd.
Think quick *pop*, yelp, then puckered fur.
Think skinny ribs. Think smell.
Think almost reaching grief, but
not quite getting there.

After Leaving McGuire Veterans' Hospital for the Last Time

This is the last place you'll ever think
you know. You would be wrong of course.
There is time enough to find
other rooms to be reminded of,
other windows to look out,
chipped sills to lean against
that rub your elbows raw. January
is not so cold here as it is elsewhere,
a little gift. When the wind blows it is
its music you remember, not its chill
as it shakes the empty branches and arrives
wherever wind arrives. Go there then, there.
Follow the long and slender blacktop as
it struggles east along the banks
through sprawling fog not destined
to survive its movement in the morning
toward the sea. And toward the sea
the sound of singing ceases, silences
beginning with a sputter and a cough
as the driver of the truck you hitchhiked in

pulls off, and one more cloud of dust
in your life of clouds of dust disintegrates
as evening settles in. What song is this?
you remember the immigrant clinician asked,
and now again along a shoreline in the night
you realize your life is just a catalog
of methods, every word of it an effort
to stay sane. Count to ten whenever
you begin to shake. If pain of any kind
is felt, take whatever is around
into your hands and squeeze, push
your feet as far as they will go
into the earth. Burial is likely what
you're after anyway. If it's unseemly,
these thoughts, or the fact that the last
unstained shirt you wore was on
a Tuesday, a week ago or more, do not
apologize. If you've earned anything
it is the right to be unseemly
while you decide at what point
the bay becomes the ocean, what
is the calculus of change required
to find what's lost if what is lost
is you. Is that a song you hear
out there, where the reeds begin
to end on every curvature of coast,
is its refrain asking what you will remember,

41

or is it saying, no, don't tell, ever?
You'll realize you're clinging
to a tree islanded amidst a brackish sea
of bulrush, the call of whip-poor-wills
and all the emptiness you asked for.
No reply: the nautilus repeats
its pattern, a line of waves
beats on forever as you enter them.
Somewhere a woman washes clothes
along the rocks. It was true
what you said. You came home
with nothing, and you still
have most of it left.

Separation

I want the boys at the end of the bar
to know, these Young Republicans
in pink popped-collar shirts, to know
that laughter drives me mad
and if one must be old
before one dies, then we were
old. Nineteen or twenty-three
and we were old and now
as the fan spins and the light
shines off their gelled hair and
nails, I want to rub their clean
bodies in blood. I want my rifle
and I want them to know
how scared I am still, alone
in bars these three years later when
I notice it is gone. I want the boys
at the end of the bar to know
that my rifle weighed eight pounds
when loaded and on my first day
home I made a scene in a bar,

so drunk that I screamed and
wept and begged for someone
to give it back. "How will I return
fire?" I cried. I truly cried.
But no one could give it back
because it was gone and I felt
so old: twenty-four and crying
for my rifle and the boys
at the end of the bar
were laughing.

Actuary

The burnt pan
I have begun to cook my bacon in
is stripped and smells somehow of lilies,
open white and wide
on the table by the window.
I do not know
why this should or should not be so.
It is just another bafflement
in a world
built out of bafflement.

Outside it is winter
once again, unseasonably warm.
The air is uniform
and I can hardly even tell
if it is inside or outside of
my body as I breathe it. If I do not
go back to it, the house will burn.

If I do not go back to it,
I will never know
what mattered.

Photographing the Suddenly Dead

Images anesthetize.

— Susan Sontag

Fact: anything invented must someday circle back
to its beginning: one puff of smoke as a lanyard
is let go, which precedes the leaning out
from underneath a hood, adapting
to the newness of the light
after so much time
in the finite darkness
that the hood had made
so carefully, as if it alone
could be the difference
between life and every other form
of composition.

Know, too, there is a photograph
at the bottom of an abandoned duffel bag
left on purpose underneath
whatever unused items

take up space
in an aging mother's
rarely opened-up garage.

At night, above it, there are stars.
I've seen them. Any claim of permanence
must kneel before this fact, and kneel too
before the puff of smoke that made
the picture happen.

What does it mean to say,
I made this? Must I claim
both the image and the act?
One, the killing
of three young men whose crime
was an unwillingness
to apply the brakes in time
to stop before arriving
at a checkpoint.

The other, a simple flash
and click, a record of
a broken arm and blood,
a rusted rifle and a shot-up car,
a certain quality of light
as it refracted through the dust
that lingered high above

the wadi where they ended up,
soon to be on fire.
Someone laughed as it was taken.
Everyone wave good-bye,
we said and laughed again
when our relief arrived.

We no longer have to name
the sins that we are guilty of.
The evidence for every crime
exists. What one
must always answer for
is not what has been done, but
for the weight of what remains
as residue — every effort
must be made to scrub away
the stain we've made on time.

Brady, for one, never made a photo
of a battle as it happened. At first,
too much stillness was required
to fix the albumin in place.
In the end the dead, unburied
and left open to the air,
were committed to the light
as it reacted to the mostly
silver nitrate mix. I wonder

if it was someone's job
to check a watch, to time it all,
or what it meant that Brady,
almost blind as war began,
would let himself go bankrupt too,
just to get the process right.

I found that it was not enough
to leave that day behind
at the bottom of a duffel bag,
or to linger in the backyard
by my mother's pond, trying to replace
what I imagined were its fading edges
with a catalog
of changing leaves in fall,
each shifting color captured
in a frame, one shutter opened
to a drowned and dying oak,
the next, the water
it was drowning in.
Nor would it be enough
to have myself for months secluded
in the dark rooms
of an apartment
I'd wound up paying for up front,
desperate for anything
to keep out light, a sometimes

loaded gun,
and whatever solitude
I needed to survive
the next unraveling,
undocumented instant.

THREE

Cumberland Gap

I first realized I was evaporating
when I was twelve, having heard

for the first time the word *embarcadero,*
from some boy leafing through a battered copy

of a triple A road atlas tucked onto a shelf,
one volume in the series of books of maps

that had for a long time composed
the section of the library devoted to geography.

It was a place, but not in any real sense
except the one I'd guessed at, the exotic newness

of a word that finished with a vowel, and if I,
in the library of a worn-out-already rural school,

created in my mind a picture that could be called
a fair approximation of the place as it existed,

the long line of the esplanade falling off
into the distances, perhaps the fine grey of

the Pacific reaching through the uncertainty of fog,
and then at night, the book of maps now left

open on a table, I could create the bustle
of a group of stars that never were. I'd be called

lucky, or just dead wrong, and for a moment,
motionless, I'd be clearly drawn to scale upon the page

with just the clarity that I had hoped for, not knowing
the fruitlessness of having clarity among one's hopes.

When the librarian called my name my name
was made into a kind of spell, dispersing everything

I could identify or claim as being part
of one certain, undisputed me, the long walk

down the hall as she held my hand, deferring
every question I might ask until a later time,

and I remember the bright red dust of dried-up clay
that swung in liquid-looking rivulets as I sat

in the parking lot and waited for my father's Chevy to appear,
knowing only that someone was dying, thinking only

of the word *embarcadero,* any place other than the place
I was forced to occupy in time and space, any name

of any town whose weight could be abandoned
with enough repeating, and giving up at last, the last

of the other children gone, hearing in my father's voice
his philosophy of living, always buy a Chevy, son,

those goddamn Fords are designed for obsolescence,
the plan, see, is in five years it'll break down

and you'll have to buy another, and I asked if it was like
the broken bicycle he'd bought for me that we'd repaired

one piece at a time until it worked, how when
we screwed the last bolt onto the new sprocket

the old bike was no longer there, everything replaced,
the broken pieces set aside and what did it mean,

and his face, which I remember over everything, lined
with a map-like certainty of shame because he had no answer,

offered none, and then the tracks of the Chevy's tires
turned up the dust again, the pine trees bright and
   luminous

with their late spring blanketing of pollen underneath
the unreal quality of light in which we lived, until I climbed

into the seat beside him, that rag he had
by then begun to cough into
already resting on his knee.

The Torch and Pitchfork Blues

Whoever picks up the last of the thrown jacks
while the ball still bounces off the pavement
and hangs suspended in the kicked-up playground dust
must also retrieve the history of the ground
where it will land. There are rules. Tell us,
boy, called out on eenie, if you
have guessed them yet. Before there was
brushed nickel there was iron, before
Tommy Dunlap was pushed idly from the bus
into that busy intersection, there was
a plenitude of grief already. Measured
against all that, a single incident recedes
into no biggie, just a memory that will help
to make his fourth-grade classmates cautious,
for a time at least, until they can no longer take
the weight of that third and fourth look down the street
when crossing into any kind of danger.
It doesn't matter, can't, and even if the impact
of that moment could be measured, we cannot say
with any certainty that Sara Albertson,

ten years after, could have resisted
making dainty track marks in the crook
of her elbow, between her toes, and I have heard,
when it was at its worst, into her eyes.

Who could have known, of the children
gathered in a circle, picking for a game of jacks,
that the ground on which they walked
had once been furrowed by a group of,
well, you-know-whos. Who among them
could have known? Well, really, any,
had they been even half-aware in class,
had they opened up their textbooks once,
had they heard their fathers say, *If them
niggers keep comin' we're leavin'.*

Without the plans for the school, now buried
in the county zoning office basement,
or some historical artifact that would give
the layout of the old plantation, it would be difficult
to say for sure if the fence they crawled under to escape
had been over by the baseball field
or by the lower meadow where the kindergarteners
played that game in gym with a parachute and tennis ball,
the children's arms just barely strong enough
to send it lofting into the blue sky, and them too young
to know not to look directly at it, yellow and hanging

as if by magic, blinding as it reached the apex
of its flight. By Christmas break they would perfect
their method, the whole game now brought indoors,
the children trained to never look again.
You might say they failed to learn the only lesson
any one of them would have ever needed since: that if
anything on earth has earned the right to be observed
it is a thing of beauty while in flight.
You might say. You might say. You might.

Fighting out of West Virginia

There he is in the blue trunks in the corner. Eyes all aflutter. His face above the blue mat and the nose not gently folded over has the crowd all saying, "Thank God for cartilage and bone," while feeling along those parts of their bodies that are as yet intact, the way people often do when confronted with disfigurement. The broken nose has earned him ten thousand dollars. Not the nose exactly, but the willingness to have it broken in the undercard fight of a second-rate toughman show held three times a year in the Bluefield High School Gymnasium. But we did not wonder at the nose. We wondered at the disappearance of the four state semifinal football banners on the wall when the lights went out, and at the PA crackling with guitar riffs and a voice saying, "Bluefield, West Virginia! Are you ready?" How it put everybody in every shellacked timber bleacher bench into a frenzy. When the woman three rows down leaned in to her friend, flipped out her bangs knowingly and said, "The whole to-do comes from Roanoke," we thought we were observers of some holy pilgrimage out of the east. Still, we did not wonder at the nose, for even in Bluefield doctors set broken bones. They come out of the mines all the time, out of the old railroad junction, sometimes out of the bars when boys from the Virginia side and boys from the West Virginia side start hollering into the streets on account of someone taking the name West by God Virginia in vain. And this boy, lying in the blue trunks in the corner, is no stranger to being broken. If we'd seen his face before the fight, if it had not been obscured by the flash of cheap carnival strobes, we would have seen the nose sitting on top of his face all askew like a shoal sticking out of the New River in the dry season. After the fight, the fine lights shipped in from Roanoke rest before the headline bout. The gym is illuminated only by its local splendor and the janitor in that yellow pall pushes a dry broom through the blood, the lines rough and straight across the mat like some misplaced Zen garden. And if we look at him in the corner, eyes still fluttering, we might also notice a tremor running from foot to ankle to knee. We might notice a few teeth dotting the dry-broomed blood beside him on the mat. We might look again at his eyes fluttering now, and because wonder is by no means married to consciousness, we might think of his sister waiting at the Travel America on Interstate 81, how she does not need ten thousand, only ten or twenty, because she has worked her way from OxyContin to meth. We might see her eyes fall on their father's shaving strop, the shine dulling both love and luster from the father's eyes before he raises up his hand with it. We might lastly stare out at this boy in the blue trunks in the corner as they carry him off with his nose broken and a little of his blood spilled out before hearing the announcer say, "Ladies and gentlemen, a hand for the loser, fighting out of West Virginia." And it will be no great wonder to us that he smiles.

In the Ruins of the Ironworks

We had been looking for a sign and there it was:
the faded copper explaining that the iron of this place
was once known throughout
the South;
the nails, the pins, the wire; the things with which
to make machines; gleaming
instruments to single-row plow
the earth.
And past the sign: into the faint greased lubricant
smell of the foundry; into the crumbling
buildings,
where men once turned black from the smoke
that escaped the flues and made their bodies be
striped with soot
and sweat
as they smelted ingots, black and hot as the air
that rattled in their lungs
to give us
industry.
If, even past these remnants, we could see

the hill and the quarried stone where they perched
two cannons overlooking
the low river,
and the rocks, graffiti-covered and vast,
perhaps we truly would be told
that Michael still loves
Lou-Anne,
even if it was for only one night, with black
enamel spray paint in the heat
of a July evening
that they stroked and burned through
in '83.

Songs in Planck Time

I rank first among all things
the new pine board

my father and I nailed
into the half-collapsing dock

that lurched out back then
when I was young

into the brackish end of the Mattaponi.
I seem to recall something obvious

about the way that one board
was devoid of natural qualities, was

out of place and undeveloped in time, was
as yet unweathered as was I, the reverse

of which is mere endurance, an impotent
going on; so add it to the list

of things that I am not, if something must
be done with it:

not the prince of any
even minor island. Not

and won't be the hero of anybody's story
but my own, if that. Not

the ripple moving outward, not
the flat of the oar that slapped the water,

not the sound it made that drove
every bird from every branch at once, not

the sky they darkened with
their flight. Not

my memory of you still on that long
walk to the end of the dock,

jumping over every missing timber
as if it might make a bit of difference when

you spread out your arms and paused, then
finally fell into the water. Not

even briefly any father's son, not any
song we haven't heard before.

The Abhorrence of Coincidence

Look, out there
that goddamn lame horse
kicks up just the most recent of
the newly dusted snow,

which forms into a pattern,
a small ellipsis underneath
the lightning-split dogwood tree
you tried to mend
with wood glue, bandages,
and a spool of rusty bailing wire,

the end result of which
was nothing more than a dead tree
adorned with the trappings
of some god-awful human injury.

You are out back by the barn now,
hammering nails into
eighty dollars' worth of shoes

for that damn horse
you said we shouldn't kill,

and I tap my finger on the window,
and see myself mirrored in
the nails you drove already,
and in the manner of the impertinent roan
who ran in circles in the snow
this afternoon and made
the dirt turn up, who turned
the snow a little brown, the one
you always lectured me about
never trying to ride.

I remember when we had
no horse, no pasture
in which it could trample earth
into a name, or if not a name
something that would instigate
my thinking on the time
I said your name

over and over again
as if it might be made
into a kind of destiny,
a destiny of saying, and being
said, and by me, as if

a pale ellipsis could of its own accord
resist its being covered
by a lame horse turning up
the dirt a little more,

and so I write your name now
in the breath I've left against
the glass, the need for tapping
gone, the surprise long passed
from your saying in the night
not names but something else,
not destiny but, *Hell, if I was anywhere*
but here I'd be just as much in love
with someone else,

and so I breathe again
and cover up
your name,
for I am not anywhere,
and I am not else.

While Trying to Make an Arrowhead in the Fashion of the Mattaponi Indians

We are born to be makers of crude tools.
And our speech is full of cruel
signifiers: you, me, them, us. I
am sure we will not survive.

No. I am only certain that the
pine trees that ring this lake in Virginia
are occasional, that I sit between them
at the water's edge,

cast two stones against
each other and rest.
For we go down
through these
terrible hours
together.

FOUR

The Locks of the James

History isn't over, in spite of our desire
for it to be. Even now, one can see
the windfall of leaves gathering
like lost baggage on the dirty pathways
paralleling the old canal, itself resurrected
in an attempt to reproduce a minor economic miracle
that had taken place in a similarly middling city
halfway across this continent. I walked the route
with my father on the day of its opening,
before the new commercial ventures gained
brief fame and the shops and music halls,
the apartments in the husks of once burnt
tobacco warehouses collectively became
the place to be. He pointed out the sheer scale
of the endeavor, the countless men it took to dig
the channels, the drivers of the boats, the ingenuity
of fixing all the mechanisms in place without
the aid of welding. A scale model of the working locks
could be operated by inserting a penny in a slot.

Two doors shut, the lower chamber filled
with water, ostensibly bringing a ship
laden with goods to the level of the next
enclosure, where it could, by all accounts,
navigate the waters beyond the fall line
out even to Ohio, with luck, beyond
the Mississippi. I only later learned
the scale model of the locks I'd played with
was the only working set the river had ever known,
the actual project having run into financial troubles,
driven into the ground by every brand
of huckster and charlatan one could imagine,
not to mention the fact that the railroads
had already made ten thousand men's lifework
obsolete. And I wonder if I should be angry
that my father never mentioned this, that instead
of acknowledging the fact that this project had failed,
had been utterly doomed from the start, he'd made
a big production over the model boat that had gone
missing from the little plastic locks. What would he
have told me, as we sat carving newer, better boats
from peels of silver birch bark? What would he
have said as we watched the water raise them
and the doors to all that was beyond opened triumphantly
and we walked the three or four steps to the end
of the display, then started over? Anger
seems absurd, but so too does this effort

to recollect, to reconstruct a moment from my life
in miniature, knowing that a scale model can accomplish
nothing when the life-sized thing was never built,
knowing that everything in the world only reminds me
of something else. The last time I went
the whole lot of it had been abandoned, more or less.
A few bums hadn't gotten the message
that the civic venture was a failure, one or two
unremarkable concerts had occurred, a couple of yuppies
were still rumored to be living, all alone, in the penthouse
apartment of a renovated tobacco warehouse, there was
a stink about a parking lot that had been laid
over a slave burial ground. Nevertheless,
the sun was bright in the sky and the bums
dangled their fingertips in the canal's green water,
and apparently some landlord was still paying
to have the grass kept green and mowed.
My father had been buried not far
from there. No one sang at his wake.
The absence seemed improper, deep in misery or not,
like it was just as well for us to see song
buried with him. I passed the statue
of Christopher Newport as I left, as I had
that day with my father. I can't recall
feeling any different, though I probably did,
having learned in the intervening period that besides
being an accidental founder of this city, he was also

a pirate and a murderer of indigenous peoples.
If I'm honest, I don't think I cared.
If I'm honest, mine is the only history
that really interests me, which is unfortunate,
because I am not alone.

Church Hill

Watch how the drivers on the hill
make a blinking semaphore
of hazard lights, car horns and the idle
movement of their engines,
and pause beside the church
that gave the hill its name,
from which you once could see
the river and a city built
at a bend which reminded
some back then of another
on the Thames. So much
is made of likenesses.

Now a parade of candles held aloft are cupped
with a reverence for the melted wax
as the candles disappear to nubs.
There is an earnestness of being there
that I can't understand.

Some say only vigils are alarming now;
each cause for grief becomes
a public play, improving on the passé
tragedy of dirt. If you undress
the earth right here, attempt
to excavate the hill, you will find
that every human wish
is buried there, underneath
the Georgian houses, under too
the veneer of asphalt
that hides a catalog of graves
the paraders somehow still recall,
perhaps with a sense
that there is imperfection
in anything that's made,
or that the alleged ghosts
are all that remain
of an abandoned field hospital,
where now there is a sketchy park
with a seesaw and a too-loose set
of monkey bars, where once
there was a pile of discarded limbs
stacked to the exact height at which
they could hold themselves aloft.
An entire train was later buried
underneath the hill. A tunnel,

poorly built, collapsed. At some point
everyone stopped trying
to dig the survivors out and went back
to whatever it was they'd done before,
despite the fact that witnesses attest
to having heard, for days after,
a muffled noise that seemed
to mimic human speech,
and later still, the quiet ringing
of the Pullman's bell.
Everything's exhausting.
No one should be blamed for this.

The parade is over anyway.
All that's left of whatever grief there was
is the splotchy wax of melted candles,
some plastic cups tossed into a gutter,
a line of cars disappearing into other
darknesses, the echo in the church
of the reenacted speech that Patrick Henry gave
making a nation out of violence.
If I remember right the church bell rang.
Everything was silent
to the west.

Nominally

Every beginning is just a course correction,
the loosest string of the as yet untangled knot, the last
thought not yet lost and so worth playing out
as I wait for some new sadness to begin.
As in, down in the valley where I'm from there is
a parking lot, which covers up a grave,
a name we give in singular for the hundred slaves
they buried there back then. And I am unmoved by the cold
cardinality of this, and all the marks the waves
wore into the outer walls of factories
when the last flash flood that briefly threatened us
came through in '98. I stand beneath the interstate
as it rumbles overhead and disappears.
There were some names here once.
Some children, too. So what? Nothing
was counted. Order is a myth.

Corona

Four p.m., Late Empire, the historians will write,
the child on the banks of the James
creating a kingdom in his mind
first brings tyranny into the realm
at the end of a kite string, tugging
it this way and that, disinterestedly,
until the kite moving across the sky
becomes a symbol of abjection,
a disgrace, and is hated by the kingdom's
living god and only subject. In none
of the many volumes written in the boy king's honor
do they mention the ball of infant snakes
that startled him by drifting out from under
the log on which he stood, causing him
to let loose the string of the kite, but then again,
neither do they tell of the great fire that began
a hundred and fifty years before in a tobacco warehouse
across from where he stood and spread
to every corner of the city until the glow
of the remaining embers was seen

as an ominous beacon by the rebel lookouts on Spy Rock,
a point two hundred miles or more to the west
in the Appalachian Mountains. Shrug,
if you must; history is made of such omissions.
If we had paid more attention
we would not know more. If we were distracted
in the middle kingdom by a cloud
passing over the sun, obscuring
our view of the kite and the city skyline,
now rebuilt, as was the king in his regal isolation,
it would be understood as a natural failing,
one that would perhaps imbue our lives
with greater meaning, but it would not be true.
We would not know how the boy king,
years later, without heirs, would consider
his reign a failure, for how brief it was, an hour,
at best an afternoon, at worst the time it took
for that cloud to pass and dissipate, and he
would watch himself walk down the cobblestone streets,
the lamps forever gaslit, the footpaths of his life
as yet unweathered by the soles of his imagined subjects'
feet, nor by the pair of egrets who flapped their wings above
the river, nor by the long carp swimming out where it became
a brackish estuary, nor by the kite
flown off into the unverifiable distances.

An Alternate History of the
Destruction of Dresden by Fire

"Them that dwell carelessly, rejoice!" the headline said.
 Saying not that
the deaf child lived, but died a moment after seeing the
 planes' stark gleam.

The bombers' bombs fell past the gunners in their balls, as
 each tallied his
mission and each thought was released once fell. Below in
 Dresden it was cold

and the breath of the citizens and the breath of zoo animals
 stirred skyward
like steam rising in cadence from this strange menagerie
 that breathed.

Even the deaf child thought he felt the thunder of a hum
 and stood, signing
to the zookeeper, signing to his parents *"Was ist das?"* as
 they turned west

and watched the sky fill up with bright, metallic, February
   reflections
of the sun off planes. Past the Elbe the sky filled with a
   thousand tired

boys from Richmond, boys from Birmingham, from Detroit
   and York,
holding their breath as the flak exploded all around and
   they waited

to die. Seconds below, the deaf child smiled and turned to a
   brown bear
pacing through the new mute snow and said *"Bär, ich höre!"*

before he seared through the sound of Dresden burning
and a cub was born crying: toothless, blind and bald.

Portugal

When my mother spoke she gave
me consciousness. The black sight of

cormorants nesting in rocks, sea-beat
and flowering out of green water,

knees me to earth. Thus was I taught
to pray—root your knees in the earth.

Between clasped fingers I see the sun
fall into the Atlantic and am afraid.

Red, like a wound bled into water,
mixes with my mother's voice,

Não há bela sem senão. I am told
those words were first to reach my ears

but mine was a murdering birth. When I look
into the ocean I am afraid. When I turn

to my mother's grave, a hole in the dirt
beneath cork oak and wheat, I am afraid

because the edge of a peninsula is a great mass
of earth — so much to put my mother in,
so much with which to cover her.

Advice to Be Taken Just Before the Sun Goes Supernova

Take three buses anywhere.
Ignore the location of each transfer.
Be prepared to exit any one of them
at random. Everyone is where they are
by accident; they will likely be as scared
as you are. Try to have your thoughts by chance.
Remember the encrypted book by Bacon
that you heard of once, how its
calfskin pages held a perfect drawing
of cells at magnification and three nudes
dancing in a ring around the edges
of the page. No one's ever going to read it.
Step out onto the dirty skin
of town again. Think of how each city
that you've been in seems the same.
There, a building tilted to appease
the ego of an old unnoticed architect.
Here, a man, you, turning to look
at trash collecting in the intersections.
Nothing changes. Each way you look

there is a toll, within each booth
a man sits behind a curtain, behind
each window you are reflected
in an oddly overlapping way,
you find a tunnel and shout to hear
the sound of your voice echo off its echo
as if to verify that you are more than just
another piece of sacking added to the swirl
of forgotten objects swinging round
a million little masses we can't see;
but you are not, and I promise
someone will love you anyway.

A Lamp in the Place of the Sun

A complete picture of the universe
as it currently exists
is not impossible,
only difficult. The warmth
of any kind of light
is just an effigy of history,
each star the record of
a million, million cities
waiting to be burned
and lived in once again.
And farther into all
our darkened rooms
we go, as though in them
we might remember
something: where it was
we left the house key,
who it was that slept
in the small ocean of our bed,
and why we loved
their sleeping, why the door

seems different now
and unafraid
of being opened.
How long I waited
for the end of winter.
How quickly I forgot
the cold when it was over.

Grace Note

It's time to take a break from all that now.
No use the artifacts
from which I've built the buried outline of a life,
no use the broken breath
which I recall from time to time
still rattles in my chest. Yes, we're due:
a break from everything, from use,
from breath, from artifacts, from life,
from death, from every unmoored memory
I've wasted all those hours upon
hoping someday something will make sense:
the old man underneath the corrugated plastic
awning of the porch, drunk and slightly
slipping off into the granite hills
of southeast Connecticut already, the hills sheaved off
and him sheaved off and saying
(in reply to what?) "Boy, that weren't nothing
but true facts about the world."
That was it. The thing I can't recall
was what I had been waiting for.

It likely won't come back again.
And I know better than to hope,
but one might wait
and pay attention
and rest awhile,
for we are more than figuring the odds.

ACKNOWLEDGMENTS

I'd like to take this opportunity to express my thanks to the magazines and journals that previously published some of the poems in this collection. I am also grateful to the faculty and staff at both the Michener Center for Writers and Virginia Commonwealth University, especially Jordan Rice, Gary Sange, Dean Young, and Jim Magnuson. To the many friends who read some or all of these poems, I say thanks, and thanks most of all to Carolina Ebeid, Shamala Gallagher, and Leanna Petronella. I have had the good fortune to work on this collection with a number of extraordinary people at Little, Brown and Company, including Victoria Matsui, Michael Pietsch, Nicole Dewey, and Morgan Moroney. Also, to everyone at RCW, especially Peter Straus, your friendship and guidance are both buoying and indispensable. Finally, to my wife and family, all my love, forever.

ABOUT THE AUTHOR

Kevin Powers is the author of the novel *The Yellow Birds,*
which was a National Book Award finalist, a PEN/Hemingway
Award winner, and a Guardian First Book Award winner.
Powers was born and raised in Richmond, Virginia, graduated
from Virginia Commonwealth University, and holds an MFA
from the University of Texas at Austin, where he was a
Michener Fellow in Poetry. He served in the U.S. Army in 2004
and 2005 in Iraq, where he was deployed as a machine gunner
in Mosul and Tal Afar. This is his first collection of poetry.